# Unfinished

# UNFINISHED

### The Four Callings
### *from* Jesus That
### Empower *and* Complete
### Your Purpose *on* Earth

# STEVEN K.
# SCOTT

### WATERBROOK
PRESS

Adapted from *The Jesus Mission*

UNFINISHED
PUBLISHED BY WATERBROOK PRESS
12265 Oracle Boulevard, Suite 200
Colorado Springs, Colorado 80921

All Scripture quotations, unless otherwise indicated, are taken from the Holy Bible, New International Version®, NIV®. Copyright © 1973, 1978, 1984 by Biblica Inc.™ Used by permission of Zondervan. All rights reserved worldwide. www.zondervan.com. Scripture quotations marked (KJV) are taken from the King James Version. Scripture quotations marked (NKJV) are taken from the New King James Version®. Copyright © 1982 by Thomas Nelson Inc. Used by permission. All rights reserved.

Italics in Scripture quotations reflect the author's added emphasis.

Details in some anecdotes and stories have been changed to protect the identities of the persons involved.

Hardcover ISBN: 978-0-307-73170-8
eBook ISBN: 978-0-307-73172-2

Cover design by Mark D. Ford

Adapted from *The Jesus Mission,* copyright © 2011 by Steve Scott, published by WaterBrook Press.

Published in the United States by WaterBrook Multnomah, an imprint of the Crown Publishing Group, a division of Random House Inc., New York.

WATERBROOK and its deer colophon are registered trademarks of Random House Inc.

Library of Congress Cataloging-in-Publication Data
Scott, Steve, 1948-
  Unfinished : the four callings from Jesus that empower and complete your purpose on earth / Steven K. Scott. — First Edition.
    pages cm
  Includes bibliographical references.
  ISBN 978-0-307-73170-8 — ISBN 978-0-307-73172-2
  1. Christian life. I. Title.
  BV4501.3.S39356 2013
  248.4—dc23

                                                              2012048618

Printed in the United States of America
2013—First Edition

10 9 8 7 6 5 4 3 2 1

SPECIAL SALES
Most WaterBrook Multnomah books are available at special quantity discounts when purchased in bulk by corporations, organizations, and special-interest groups. Custom imprinting or excerpting can also be done to fit special needs. For information, please e-mail SpecialMarkets@WaterBrookMultnomah.com or call 1-800-603-7051.

And this is eternal life, that they may know You, the only true God, and Jesus Christ whom You have sent.

—JESUS (JOHN 17:3, NKJV)

# CONTENTS

# JESUS GIVES HIS FOLLOWERS FOUR CALLINGS

*(And with Each Calling, He Gives an Unimaginable Gift)*

As my Father hath sent me,
even so send I you.
—JOHN 20:21 (KJV)

From the beginning of His ministry on earth, Jesus told His followers that He was sent to this world by His Father in heaven. That concept is fundamental to Christianity. If you ask a Christian, "Why did the Father send His Son into this world?" he or she might first say, "To die on the cross as the perfect Sacrifice for our sins." Then the person might add, "And to provide God's free gift of eternal life to those who would believe in Him."

As true as these answers are, anyone who stops with these words is missing vitally important truths that Jesus revealed about the many other reasons He came to earth, including the fundamental reason: that His Father *sent* Him.

Jesus was sent to earth to accomplish nearly *thirty* specific missions. And each of the missions was assigned to

Him by the Father before Christ left heaven (John 5:36; 6:38). The Father also gave Jesus the exact messages He wanted Jesus to communicate to the world—down to the very words He was to speak.

Jesus told His followers, "For I did not speak of my own accord, but the Father who sent me commanded me what to say and how to say it" (John 12:49). (See also John 8:26–29; John 14:24.) All of this makes it clear that Jesus didn't come here just to go with the flow or to fulfill a single, general purpose. He came to accomplish every aspect of every mission that His Father commanded Him to accomplish, and to say every word the Father told Him to say.

Jesus came to finish the work of His Father on earth (John 4:34; 5:36).

## THE MOST IMPORTANT QUESTIONS YOU CAN ASK

If God had such specific purposes for Jesus, does He also have specific purposes and callings that He wants you to accomplish? Jesus answered this question in John 20:21 when He told His closest followers, "As the Father has sent Me, I also send you" (NKJV). Jesus sends His followers into the world in the same manner that His Father sent Him. Jesus has given us four specific callings, and we are to focus on accomplishing them.

We are not to walk casually through life, reacting to whatever might come along. Jesus tells us to never allow our lives to be determined by circumstances. Rather, He wants us to passionately pursue—and accomplish—the callings He has set before us.

Thus, the two most important questions you can ask are

1. What callings has Jesus given me?
2. How can I fulfill those callings and accomplish the related missions?

The good news is that Jesus answered both questions in very specific terms. Equally important, He promised that if you would pursue the callings and missions He has revealed, the Holy Spirit would give you the miraculous power to accomplish them. Along with every calling, Jesus gives us the gifts that are needed to pursue and accomplish the calling.

Jesus revealed four callings that we are to embrace as our top priorities in life. The callings make God's will for each of us crystal clear. As we pursue each one in faith, the Holy

Spirit will perform His miraculous transformational power in our lives and in the lives of the people we serve. With a clear understanding of what Christ left for us to do on earth, we can make the most of every miraculous, eternal opportunity that God brings into our lives.

# ONE

# THE FIRST GIFT
# AND CALLING

*Become More Intimate
with God*

God desires to have intimacy with us and for us to live in an intimate relationship with Him. The pursuit of this first of our four callings is how we bless God. It also captures the number-one priority for our lives—given to us by God.

In Jeremiah 9:23–24, God said, "Let not the wise man glory in his wisdom, let not the mighty man glory in his might, nor let the rich man glory in his riches; but let him who glories glory in this, that he understands and [intimately] knows Me, that I am the LORD, exercising lovingkindness, judgment, and righteousness in the earth. For in these I delight" (NKJV). And in John 17:3, Jesus said, "And this is eternal life, that they may [intimately] know You, the only true God, and Jesus Christ whom You have sent" (NKJV). As we pursue intimacy with God as a means to bless Him, He gives us the greatest gift we can receive—true intimacy with Him.

Our first calling, to grow always in deeper intimacy with God, is also His greatest gift to us during our lives on earth. Everything we will become and everything we achieve that is of eternal worth is dependent on God's grace and our level of intimacy with Him. In the fourteenth chapter of John, Jesus gives us the key to pursuing and achieving intimacy with God. To draw near to God and to live our lives in an intimate relationship with Him, we must love God the way *He* wants to be loved. Loving God does not involve generating an emotional feeling that we identify as love for Him. Instead, Jesus tells us that we love God by obeying the teachings and commands of Christ. The promised gift, in return for that obedience, is a level of intimacy with Him that goes beyond anything we can imagine.

Jesus has told us:

He who has My commandments and keeps them, it
is he who loves Me. And he who loves Me will be
loved by My Father, and I will love him and manifest
Myself to him.… If anyone loves Me, he will keep
My word; and My Father will love him, and We will

come to him and make Our home with him. (John 14:21, 23, NKJV)

Unlike the commands of the Law, the teachings and commands of Christ are not burdensome (1 John 5:3). They accomplish three things with unparalleled clarity and power:

1. They reveal the true realities of our moment-by-moment circumstances from God's perspective.
2. They reveal God's perfect will for every circumstance we find ourselves in and for every decision and choice we face.
3. They become the tools the Holy Spirit uses to empower us to follow God's will in any situation.

If we do not experience intimacy with God, all our efforts to achieve results of eternal worth will fail. Jesus made this clear: "I am the vine, you are the branches. He who abides in Me, and I in him, bears much fruit; for without Me you can do *nothing*" (John 15:5, NKJV). When Jesus said "nothing," He meant it. Of course, we can still tell others about Christ and go through the motions of living the Christian life. But if we do not live in an intimate relationship with Christ, none of our efforts will produce fruit of eternal value.

So the first call Christ gave us focuses on our relationship with the Father and the Son. To pursue and accomplish this calling, there are six assignments to focus on.

## Assignment 1: Fear God

Do not be afraid of those who kill the body but cannot kill the soul. Rather, be afraid of the One who can destroy both soul and body in hell. Are not two sparrows sold for a penny? Yet not one of them will fall to the ground apart from the will of your Father. And even the very hairs of your head are all numbered. So don't be afraid; you are worth more than many sparrows. (Matthew 10:28–31)

Jesus tells us not to fear anyone or anything, even if they can kill us physically. Instead, we should be afraid "of the One who can destroy both soul and body in hell" (verse 28). Both the psalmist and Solomon told us that the fear of the Lord is the beginning of wisdom (Psalm 111:10; Proverbs 1:7; 9:10).

Solomon also called the fear of the Lord "a fountain of life" (Proverbs 14:27). Fearing God adds years to your life (Proverbs 10:27), it gives you strong confidence (Proverbs 3:26), and it creates a place of safe refuge (Proverbs 14:26). At the same time, fearing God teaches you to hate evil and pride (Proverbs 8:13) and to love righteousness (Proverbs 14:2).

We have been taught, wrongly, that fearing God is the same as *revering* Him. Though reverence is part of what it means to fear God, it does not capture its full meaning. The words used in the Bible that are translated "fear" or "afraid" in relation to God are *yirah* (Hebrew) and *phoebeo* (Greek), and they include the reality of being terrified.

Jesus made it clear that God is not to be taken lightly. God hates sin so much that He sacrificed His own Son as an atonement or covering for our sin. Do you fear cancer? How about a terrorist attack or an earthquake or a hurricane? Jesus commands His followers not to be afraid of such things, because they can kill nothing more than your body. But Jesus stressed that we *are* to fear God. A healthy fear of a holy God places God on the throne of our hearts. It positions us at a place of humility and worship before Him and motivates us to choose holiness over sin.

But Jesus didn't stop there. He said that once we realize that God is deadly serious about both sin and righteousness and that He must be taken seriously, we should not be afraid! Not even one sparrow falls to the ground apart from God's perfect will, and God loves us far more than He loves a sparrow.

Our fear of God puts following Him and obeying His will at the top of our list of priorities. As we fear God ahead of all else, we can have the confidence that nothing will come upon us without first passing through His loving will. Does this mean we will be spared adversity? Not at all. Jesus said, "In this world you will have trouble. But take heart! I have overcome the world" (John 16:33). And yet, because no adversity can kill our souls or derail what God has prepared for us in eternity, we have nothing to fear.

## ASSIGNMENT 2: SEEK FIRST HIS KINGDOM AND RIGHTEOUSNESS

Our natural inclination is to pursue everything else before we seek God's Kingdom and righteousness. Our activities and the way we use our time usually reflect a willingness to prioritize other things. But Jesus commands us to do something that runs counter to our natural inclination. We are told to seek the things of God above everything else (Matthew 6:33).

Why is our nature so contrary to His nature and the requirements of this second assignment? The answer is simple. Christ sees this life as merely a brief precursor to eternity—it's the "foreword" to our book of life. But because we exist in a time-limited realm, we see our lives on earth as the entire book. Even though we agree with the notion that this life is a momentary steppingstone into eternity, we act as if our day-to-day lives are what count most.

Does this mean we should quit our jobs and pull back from social engagements to free up time for prayer, Bible study, and missionary work? Not at all. Jesus never intended to remove us from the world but rather to call us to be His representatives in the world. We are to place our relationship with God and our calling as His subjects at the top of our priority lists. So our pursuit of His Kingdom and righteousness becomes the determining factor in every choice, decision, and action.

We need to review how we allocate our time and then replace activities that have no bearing on our pursuit of God with activities that accelerate our pursuit of the things that are most important to Him. And this can't happen if we don't discover, embrace, and obey the words of His Son! As we focus on the teachings of the Lord Jesus Christ, His values will become our values, and His priorities will become our priorities. As this realignment takes place, the things that are of little or no importance to Him will become of little or no importance to us.

We don't have an unlimited amount of time to do this. James tells us that our lives are like "a mist that appears... and then vanishes" (4:14). We usually treat time as if it were an ocean that won't run dry. Instead, it's like a barrel holding a limited amount of water that will never be replenished (Ephesians 5:15–17).

If we don't seek the things of God *first,* we will lose the time and opportunity to seek them at all. Nine times out of ten, we accomplish only what is at the top of our lists and never get to whatever is second. So here are two actions that will help you keep God's Kingdom at the top of your list.

## *Action: Worship and Serve the Lord Only*

Specific actions help us complete the assignments Christ gives us. As we pursue intimacy with God and seek His Kingdom and righteousness, the Lord has to be the only absolute Authority in our lives. When Satan tried to tempt Jesus by offering Him all the kingdoms of the world, Jesus knew it was impossible to serve two masters. Jesus answered Satan with a mission statement that defined His earthly life. He said, "You shall worship the LORD your God, and Him only you shall serve" (Matthew 4:10, NKJV; see also Deuteronomy 6:13).

We might assume that if this was one of Jesus's earthly missions, it is an action we need to take as well. But we don't have to rely on assumptions in this case, because we are commanded to do this in Matthew. Why? Because we are tempted to put other things—including money and material possessions—ahead of God. And unlike Jesus, we *do* fall to that temptation. That's why Jesus gave us so many warnings about money (Matthew 6:24). Jesus was not saying that we should take a vow of poverty or drop out of the world of commerce. But He knew human nature causes us to strive for more money and more things. So He warned us to guard against the tendency to allow money and posses-

sions to become our driving purpose. And in the next speci-
fied action, He told us how to do this.

## Action: Store Up Treasures in Heaven Instead of on Earth

Jesus said, "Store up for yourselves treasures in heaven, where
moth and rust do not destroy, and where thieves do not break
in and steal. For where your treasure is, there your heart will
be also" (Matthew 6:20–21). This action reveals how we can
make God our Master and limit money to the role of a servant. By setting our focus and efforts on doing things that
store up treasures in heaven, we turn away from acquiring
and hoarding treasures on earth. This is critically important
because our hearts (the core of who we are) can't avoid bond-
ing with whatever we treasure. God wants our hearts to bond
with Him and with things of eternal purpose and worth.

The solution is to store up treasures in heaven by bearing
spiritual fruit (John 15:7–8). This includes the "fruit of the
Spirit" (Galatians 5:22–23) and the fruits of extraordinary
forgiveness, mercy, and generosity. Also included is the fruit
from sharing your testimony of Christ and the good news of
the gospel.

According to Jesus, the only way to bear much fruit is to abide (or dwell) in Him and to let His words abide (or dwell) in us (John 15:5–8). There are no shortcuts. Christ is the Vine; we are the branches. His words are the only source of nutrition that provides the spirit and life to enable us to bear fruit. (Until you make discovering and doing His words a top priority, you will bear only a modest amount of fruit or none at all.)

## ASSIGNMENT 3: FOLLOW JESUS

What would happen if, instead of inviting people to pray to receive Christ, we invited them to become *followers* of Jesus Christ? That was how Jesus called His first disciples. He did not ask two fishermen named Peter and Andrew or a tax collector named Matthew to recite a prayer. He invited them to follow Him (Matthew 16:24). Those who accepted His invitation did so at great personal cost. For Peter and Andrew, it meant leaving behind their livelihood. For Matthew, it meant sacrificing a lucrative tax-collection business.

For all who chose to follow Jesus, it meant repentance,

saving faith, and giving Jesus the place of lordship over their hearts and lives. But most who heard Him walked away when they realized what following Him would cost.

And yet Jesus never changed His message to increase the number of people who would join Him. The path that leads to eternal life is straight and narrow. For Jesus to represent it any other way would have been a lie. He knew that only those who were truly born again would follow Him, and they would do so regardless of the cost. Why? Because when people are born again, their spiritual eyes are opened and they recognize that the temporary cost of following Christ is not high when compared to the riches of eternal life. The world has nothing to offer that comes close to matching the value of our souls and the worth of eternal life (Matthew 16:25–26).

Those who are born again desire to take up their crosses and follow Christ, to lose their lives in loving and serving their Savior (Matthew 16:25). We joyfully surrender our rights to everything because we seek the joy of following Him. So the question becomes, how can we fulfill the assignment of following Christ? The how-tos are found in four actions.

### Action: Hear His Words and Act on Them

Jesus said, "Everyone who hears these words of mine and puts them into practice is like a wise man who built his house on the rock. The rain came down, the streams rose, and the winds blew and beat against that house; yet it did not fall, because it had its foundation on the rock" (Matthew 7:24–25). As basic as this concept is, it is foreign to many professing Christians. Jesus made more than nineteen hundred statements that are recorded in the New Testament, but many believers are familiar with only a few of them. This is a tragedy because hearing and obeying Christ's words provide the only rock-solid foundation for a Christian's life (John 10:27).

### Action: Do the Things That Jesus Commands

The next action is closely related, and it is to obey everything that Christ commands. Obeying Christ is the way to love Him in the manner He wants to be loved. He said, "If anyone loves me, he will obey my teaching" (John 14:23). Obeying His commands gives us unparalleled opportunities to love Him with the highest form of love we can give.

## Action: Love Jesus More Than Your Family

One of Jesus's statements that used to trouble me was Matthew 10:37: "Anyone who loves his father or mother more than me is not worthy of me; anyone who loves his son or daughter more than me is not worthy of me." I couldn't honestly say that I loved Christ more than I loved members of my family. Then I realized that Jesus was not talking about our feelings. He was talking about loving Him by obeying His commands.

I love being at home with my wife and children. But there are times when I know Jesus wants me to do something else, such as preaching the gospel in another city. When I choose to follow Him, even when I would prefer to stay home with my family, I am loving Him more than my wife or children.

## Action: Take Up Your Cross and Lose Your Life for His Sake

In Matthew 10:38–39, Jesus said, "Anyone who does not take his cross and follow me is not worthy of me. Whoever finds his life will lose it, and whoever loses his life for my sake will find it." What looks like a burdensome, even depressing approach to life is in reality a glorious opportunity (see the example of Jesus as described in Philippians 2:5–8). The cross is an instrument of death, and the person carrying it has no alternative but to submit to the death that awaits him. The person who is carrying the cross also has lost all his rights, including the right to live as he chooses.

So you might ask, "How could such a way of life be glorious and joy producing?" Here is how. First, when you realize you have no rights, you lose your expectations. Self-directed expectations and an entitlement mentality are the enemies of happiness. They make it impossible to be grateful, and gratefulness is the source of happiness. At the same time, when you have no rights or expectations, you are grateful for everything God provides. Also, by dying to self and to your rights, you enter into a bond of intimacy with our Savior that provides joy that is not dependent on people or circumstances (John 7:38).

Finally, losing your life for Christ enables you to bear fruit and make your life count for eternity. Jesus said, "Unless a kernel of wheat falls to the ground and dies, it remains only a single seed. But if it dies, it produces many seeds. The man who loves his life will lose it, while the man who hates his life in this world will keep it for eternal life" (John 12:24–25).

## ASSIGNMENT 4: ACCEPT HIS YOKE

> Take my yoke upon you and learn from me, for I am gentle and humble in heart, and you will find rest for your souls. For my yoke is easy and my burden is light. (Matthew 11:29–30)

Though this assignment may appear to be the same as following Jesus, it is actually quite different. Here, Jesus invites us to come *alongside* Him and to bind ourselves *to* Him, rather than following along behind. When two oxen were yoked together, one served in the dominant role and would carry the bulk of the load, while the other would balance the load. Here the Lord tells us that when we are yoked to Him, He will do the heavy work while we walk with Him. As we walk alongside Him, He will accomplish His work through us.

### *Action: Learn from Christ*

Jesus's invitation to "learn from me" should be basic in every Christian's life, and yet for most of us it's foreign territory. To be yoked to Christ means that He is the first Person we learn from; after all, He is right next to us. To keep the yoke even, we must move with Him stride for stride. Unfortunately, we usually learn from other sources before we finally start to learn from Jesus. And yet He is the God who created the universe. Jesus is the only Person in history who is perfect in knowledge, wisdom, understanding, and truth. His words answer every question and resolve every problem.

Not only do we have His nineteen hundred recorded statements to learn from, but we also have the example of His life. His humility, His gentleness, and His love of righteousness and hatred of deceit and hypocrisy are just a few of His traits that teach us how to live.

## ASSIGNMENT 5: ASK THE LORD TO SEND OUT LABORERS

The harvest truly is plentiful, but the laborers are few. Therefore pray the Lord of the harvest to send out laborers into His harvest. (Matthew 9:37–38, NKJV)

Jesus's disciples accepted the assignment to pray for laborers. When He appeared to the disciples after His resurrection, only eleven remained. And yet it is estimated that nearly seventy years later, when the first century came to an end, more than *one million* people were following Christ. The harvest was plentiful, and the Lord answered the prayers of those who took this assignment seriously.

When was the last time you prayed that the Lord would send out laborers? What kind of revival would you see in your city, state, province, or nation if you and those you influence accepted this assignment every day? Ask the Lord to send laborers, and then watch how He begins to answer. In these troubled times, the fields are whiter than ever.

## ASSIGNMENT 6: BE ON HIGH ALERT FOR OPPORTUNITIES TO SERVE

My father served in the United States Army Air Forces during World War II. From time to time, his bomber squadron was stationed on various islands in the South Pacific, some of them only a mile or two wide and a couple of miles long. They had minimal land defenses against attacks from enemy aircraft. Many nights they slept in their flight suits in case they needed to scramble the planes at a moment's notice.

Jesus gave us a similar picture in Luke, but He used the analogy of the servants of a groom at a wedding feast. He said, "Be dressed ready for service and keep your lamps burning, like men waiting for their master to return from a wedding banquet.… It will be good for those servants whose master finds them watching when he comes" (12:35–37).

We have limited time to accomplish all that God has set before us. He wants us to take Him and the four callings He has given us seriously. When Christ returns, or if He calls us home prior to that time, it will be a joyous time for believers who have served Him right up to the moment we see Him face to face. It will be a bad time for those who acted as if they would never have to give an account of how they spent their time and resources.

Let us now turn to our second calling from Christ, that of accelerating our personal growth.

# TWO

# THE SECOND GIFT AND CALLING

*Accelerate
Your Personal Growth*

Most of us see world-class athletes only when they are competing, when they are focused completely on their events. At that moment they are thinking of nothing else but what goes into winning. What we don't see is all the preparation and training they went through to get to those events. And yet how well athletes perform is determined primarily by how well they prepared in the previous days, weeks, and months.

When my son Ryan was sixteen, he won the national championship in the high jump at the Junior Olympics. During that competition, he jumped twelve times. Each jump took six seconds from beginning to end. So in that competition, Ryan's total performance time was seventy-two seconds. To win the national championship, he had to jump higher than he had ever jumped before. And that's what he did. But the only reason he was able to qualify for that meet was that he had trained two hours a day, six days a week, for fifty weeks. *Six hundred hours* of conditioning and training for seventy-two seconds of championship performance.

As Christians, our success in ministering to others depends on our relationship with God and our spiritual growth. Unfortunately, this second calling from Christ—accelerating our personal growth—usually receives the least attention. Every aspect of our lives and ministry is impacted by how fast we grow spiritually. Jesus reveals that God wants us to "bear much fruit" (John 15:8). And the slower we grow spiritually, the less fruit we will bear.

Jesus gives us the necessary gifts to empower us to fulfill this awesome calling. He also makes this calling doable by giving us specific assignments to accomplish.

## Assignment 1: Be Set Apart as God's Possession

Scripture reveals six critical mission assignments and a number of closely related actions that position us for personal growth and spiritual maturity. The assignments begin with being set apart, or sanctified, for special use by God.

In Jesus's final prayer before He was arrested, He prayed for you and me (John 17:20). Just before that, He asked His Father to sanctify His followers by God's truth (verse 17).

The word *sanctify* is translated from the Greek root word *hagios,* which means "to set apart for an uncommon higher use." When the term is used to describe people, it implies that a person is separated from the common values of the world to be used by God as a holy vessel. When you are born again, it is God's will for you to be set apart for righteous and holy purposes.

Jesus, having lived without sin, was able to sanctify Himself, setting Himself apart unto God. But we need to be sanctified by an outside force, the Holy Spirit. And to do this, the Spirit uses the truth. Sanctifying truth can be found in two places: the Word of God and the life of Christ. Jesus claimed to be the Truth in human form (John 14:6), and He told Pontius Pilate that He came into the world to "bear witness to the truth" (John 18:37, NKJV). As we meditate on God's Word and embrace it by faith, the truth from His Word sanctifies us, setting us apart to be used by God and to be molded into a reflection of Christ (John 15:3). There is no other way to be sanctified than through the Word of God, both the living Word, which is Christ, and the written Word.

### Action: Become Mature and Complete in Your Faith

A number of Greek and Hebrew words that appear in the Bible are translated as the English word "perfect." Some of the words refer to exactness or precision. Others are synonymous with what we usually mean when we say "perfect," namely, without error or fault. But the Greek word used in Matthew 5:48 in reference to God the Father does not mean "exact" or "without error or fault." The word is *teleios*, which means "fully mature" or "complete." Jesus commands us to become mature and complete in our faith rather than remain in a state of immaturity. When we are born again, we are born as spiritual babies, and our natural tendencies are to continue to express the immature behavior of our previous way of life.

Jesus revealed how an immature faith expresses itself: "You have heard that it was said, 'Love your neighbor and hate your enemy'" (Matthew 5:43). Next, He described a mature or complete faith: "But I tell you: Love your enemies and pray for those who persecute you, that you may be sons of your Father in heaven" (verses 44–45). He further explained, "If you love those who love you, what reward will you get? Are not even the tax collectors doing that? And if you greet only your brothers, what are you doing more than others? Do not even pagans do that?" (verses 46–47). When believers act the same way unbelievers act, our faith is immature and incomplete at best.

Then Jesus referred to His command to love our enemies and pray for those who persecute us. He implied that doing such things is the expression of a mature and complete faith: "Be perfect [mature and complete], therefore, as your heavenly Father is perfect [mature and complete]" (verse 48). Mature believers love their enemies, blessing them and praying for them. Jesus does not command us to have loving feelings toward enemies and persecutors but rather to *act* in love. (Note that Jesus is instructing us in personal behavior, not collective behavior in a political or national context. Also, He is not relieving us from acting responsibly toward those who inflict harm. For instance, He is not commanding a Christian wife to ignore the behavior of an abusive husband or telling a Christian in the business world to ignore unethical employees or to turn a blind eye to illegal practices.)

We are not to allow revenge or malice to be the driving force of our behavior toward our enemies. Even when people commit the vilest offenses against us, we are to pray for them and forgive them (Luke 23:34).

## ASSIGNMENT 2: PURSUE RIGHTEOUSNESS AND GODLY BEHAVIOR

It is human nature to go with the flow, simply doing what comes naturally. And unfortunately, there is nothing natural about pursuing righteousness. Going with the flow usually plays to laziness and self-centered behavior. But Jesus calls us to swim upstream. In Matthew 5:6, He said those who "hunger and thirst for righteousness" will be satisfied. This may sound like a platitude, but in the ancient Greek, it's far more striking. The word translated as "hunger" means "famished" and "passionately craving." The word translated as "thirst" means "thirsty to the point of suffering." When you are that hungry or that thirsty, nothing is more important than obtaining food and water. So the question becomes, how can we gain that level of intensity of hunger and thirst for righteousness?

## *Action: Wake Up to Reality About Your Standing Before God*

Jesus began His Sermon on the Mount with the statement "Blessed are the poor in spirit, for theirs is the kingdom of heaven" (Matthew 5:3). The Greek word that is translated "poor" is *ptochos,* which means "destitute" or "one who has absolutely nothing." It was used to describe homeless beggars. Jesus said those who are spiritually destitute, having no spiritual worth of their own, will be truly blessed. They will possess the kingdom of heaven. Why? Because only the spiritually destitute realize they don't have any righteousness of their own. Their only hope of entering heaven is to acquire someone else's righteousness—and that Someone is Christ!

Those who realize their spiritual bankruptcy run to the foot of the cross with the hearts of beggars, desperate for mercy, forgiveness, and righteousness. They gladly exchange their sin for Christ's forgiveness.

## ASSIGNMENT 3: "COME TO ME"

Jesus said, "Come to me, all you who are weary and burdened, and I will give you rest" (Matthew 11:28). In other words, whenever you are stressed, fearful, or despairing, run to Jesus and the counsel of His words *first*...before you go anywhere else! He promises not only to relieve your fears and stress but also to personally carry your burden. Our nature is to turn to anyone and everyone *other* than Jesus for counsel and relief. But Jesus, through His nineteen hundred statements in the Gospels, not only answers every question and issue we will ever face, but He provides the power we need to overcome any circumstance. We know that nothing creates more stress and weariness than our sin. And Christ is the only One who can lift that burden from our hearts.

## ASSIGNMENT 4: "LEARN FROM ME"

Here is the next assignment. Jesus said, "Learn from me" (Matthew 11:29). We are to study His life and learn from

His example, and we are to meditate on His words and learn from His teachings. If we do, the Holy Spirit will use Christ's life and words to empower and accelerate our spiritual growth. This is the practical way to pursue righteousness and godly behavior. In Christ's words we find the perfect commands that unerringly reveal the ways in which we are to walk. By learning from His example and abiding in His words, we discover the Truth, which sets us free from enslavement to sin (John 8:31–36).

### Action: Pursue Inner Righteousness Without Hypocrisy

Jesus told His disciples, "I tell you that unless your righteousness surpasses that of the Pharisees and the teachers of the law, you will certainly not enter the kingdom of heaven" (Matthew 5:20). To those who heard these words in the first century, this statement would have been devastating. The Pharisees and teachers of the Law were known for their strict adherence to the letter of the Levitical laws. Certainly Jesus's disciples wondered how their own righteousness could ever surpass this.

Later, Jesus put assumptions about human righteousness

in perspective. He told the Pharisees, "Woe to you, teachers of the law and Pharisees, you hypocrites!… On the outside you appear to people as righteous but on the inside you are full of hypocrisy and wickedness" (Matthew 23:27–28). The only kind of righteousness that counts is righteousness that comes from the heart, and that kind of righteousness can only come when your heart is redeemed through Christ's atonement. When the Holy Spirit dwells within you, you experience a new level of righteousness that He expresses through you (Galatians 5:22–23).

## Action: Remove from Your Life Anything That Causes You to Fall

When I was in college, Dr. James Borror, my pastor at Scottsdale Bible Church, gave a sermon on the Lord's Prayer (Matthew 6:9–13). When he came to verse 13—"And lead us not into temptation, but deliver us from evil" (KJV)—he said he believed that we could avoid so much needless temptation if we would pray the Lord's Prayer every day from the heart.

In this same vein Jesus said, "If your right eye causes you to sin, gouge it out and throw it away. It is better for you to lose one part of your body than for your whole body to be thrown into hell. And if your right hand causes you to sin, cut it off and throw it away. It is better for you to lose one part of your body than for your whole body to go into hell" (Matthew 5:29–30). If anything in our activities or life-styles brings a level of temptation we can't handle, we should cut out the troublesome activity.

Most of the activities and influences that tempt us come through our visual and tactile appetites. If we struggle with Internet pornography, for instance, we should make sure we are never alone at a computer. Or we should install a filter and have our spouse or someone else act as administrator. By cutting off a problem at its source, we can eliminate the opportunity for temptation.

### Action: Develop and Maintain a Grateful Spirit

Christians should be the happiest people on the planet. Why? Because gratefulness is the key to happiness, and Christians have more to be thankful for than anyone else. Jesus said we should rejoice because our names are "written in heaven" (Luke 10:20). But you might be thinking that if I were familiar with your circumstances, I would understand your struggle with gratitude.

Most people let their circumstances determine their happiness or unhappiness. When things go great, they are happy, and when things go wrong, they lose their peace of mind. But for the person who lives in an intimate relationship with God, circumstances do not determine his or her gratitude.

In Luke 10, Jesus sent seventy men into surrounding towns and villages, telling them to heal the sick and preach the gospel. When they returned, they reported back to Him, "Lord, even the demons are subject to us in Your name" (verse 17, NKJV). Jesus told them, "I saw Satan fall like lightning from heaven. Behold, I give you the authority to trample on serpents and scorpions, and over all the power of the enemy, and nothing shall by any means hurt you" (verses 18–19, NKJV). And then Christ revealed the most important revelation on happiness: "Nevertheless do not rejoice in this, that the spirits are subject to you, but rather rejoice because your names are written in heaven" (verse 20, NKJV).

It is clear that not even the fact that demonic spirits were subject to them should be the source of their rejoicing. Instead, only one thing should form the basis of their rejoicing—that their names are written in heaven. The things

Jesus told His followers apply to us also. We should base our rejoicing on three truths.

First, the fact that we are going to heaven is evidence of God's greatest miracle. He transferred all our sin and its debt to His own dear Son. He transferred all of Christ's righteousness to us. He made us, people who were dead in sin, alive in Christ.

Second, when we were dead in our sins, we were born again by God's ultimate act of grace. Because of God's action, we were forgiven of our sins and redeemed by the shed blood of God's Son. Oh, what a Savior! Oh, what grace! Knowing this, how could we ever fail to be grateful?

Finally, while everything else we possess can be lost or taken away, eternal life can never be taken away. Does this mean we can't be sad or grieve? Not at all. Whenever we lose anyone or anything that is dear to us, of course we will grieve. Jesus wept at the thought of Lazarus's death even though He was only minutes away from raising him from the dead. But even when we experience sadness, we still can rejoice in the fact that we have eternal life. Rejoicing is an action inspired by faith. It is a means by which we express thanks to God for His love, mercy, forgiveness, and salvation. .

When the source of your rejoicing is the fact that you have eternal life, you can go through anything. Jesus said to His disciples, "Blessed are you when people insult you, persecute you and falsely say all kinds of evil against you because of me. Rejoice and be glad, because great is your reward in heaven" (Matthew 5:11–12). Even when we are abused by others, we can rejoice.

## Action: Don't Give In to Fear

We live in a culture permeated with anxiety. Failing economies, terrorism, violent crime, joblessness, and the rising cost of living are just a few of the circumstances that can make even the most stout-hearted become fearful. And yet Jesus commanded us not to fear. He told His disciples, "In this world you will have trouble. But take heart! I have overcome the world" (John 16:33).

It is one thing to know that Jesus tells you not to fear. But how can you be delivered from fears and anxieties? The answers are found in six steps that the Savior asks us to take.

*Step 1: Take charge of your heart.* Remember, your heart is not just your emotions; it is the core of who you are. Human nature influences you to allow outside forces to control your heart. People talk about "falling in love" as if we have no control over the process. We often blame our anger on others, just as we allow adversity, uncertainty, or fear to take charge of our hearts.

But in John 14:1 and 14:27, Jesus told His disciples, "Do not let not your hearts be troubled." He was telling them, "Wrest your heart away from the circumstances and fear that control it. Don't simply go with the flow." But once you've taken charge of your heart, how can you prevent it from falling back under the control of fear or other influences?

*Step 2: Trust in the Father and the Son.* It's easy to believe we are self-sufficient, but we are not capable of protecting our hearts. Adverse circumstances and fear are like schoolyard bullies, and we are like ninety-pound weaklings. Your only hope is to turn your heart and its protection over to Someone a lot stronger and more powerful than life's bullies.

Jesus gave us the secret to guarding our hearts: "Trust in God; trust also in me" (John 14:1). When you pass your heart over to the Father and the Son, you win and the bullies are left powerless. Our security and trust start with hearing His voice and following Him (John 10:27–29). Jesus has given us more than 100 promises and more than 140 commands. We put our trust in Him when we hear His word and by faith do what He says. Trusting Him is not a feeling; it's an action in response to His word or His prompting.

*Step 3: Be courageous.* After Jesus fed five thousand men and the women and children who were with them, He told His disciples to get into a boat and cross a lake. Then He dismissed the crowd and climbed a hill to get alone to pray. About three o'clock in the morning, the boat was far from shore and making slow progress due to high winds and rough seas. Suddenly the disciples saw an image approaching on the water. They screamed in terror, thinking it was a ghost. Then they heard Jesus say, "Take courage! It is I. Don't be afraid" (Matthew 14:27). When they heard His words, their fears were relieved.

The words from the Savior vaporized their fears. A simple statement sandwiched between two commands changed their hearts. The commands were "Take courage" and "Don't be afraid." But the statement in the middle was what empowered the disciples: "It is I." The only reason for them to be courageous was that Jesus had come to them.

No matter what we go through, as soon as we receive a word from Jesus, we realize that our world is not out of control. Jesus is close at hand, and peace will replace our fears. Adversity tests and refines our faith. The source of courage and faith are the words of Christ that assure our hearts that He is present. And because Christ reminds us that He is with us, we have no reason to fear.

*Step 4: Stop doubting and start believing.* On the day of Jesus's resurrection, some of the disciples were hiding behind locked doors. Without opening the door, Jesus appeared in their midst. However, Thomas was not there, and when the others told him later that they had seen the Lord, Thomas was doubtful. "Unless I see the nail marks in his hands and put my finger where the nails were, and put my hand into his side, I will not believe it" (John 20:25).

A week later they were together, and this time Thomas was with them. The apostle John recorded what happened. "Though the doors were locked, Jesus came and stood among them and said, 'Peace be with you!' Then he said to Thomas, 'Put your finger here; see my hands. Reach out your hand and put it into my side. Stop doubting and believe.' Thomas said to him, 'My Lord and my God!' Then

Jesus told him, 'Because you have seen me, you have believed; blessed are those who have not seen and yet have believed'" (John 20:26–29).

Jesus told Thomas (and you and me) to stop doubting and to believe. And Christ provided a detail just for us: For those who have not physically seen the Lord, when we replace doubt with belief, He will bless us in an added way. He will show us a way to love God and bless Him with a level of faith that would not be possible if we could see Him.

*Step 5: Don't worry about your life, food, or shelter.* If ever there was a command and a promise from the Lord that we ignore, it's this one! In Matthew 6:25, Jesus said, "Therefore I tell you, do not worry about your life, what you will eat or drink; or about your body, what you will wear." He began the statement with "therefore," which means that what He said previously (in verse 24) is the foundation of our ability to stop worrying. Simply stated, Jesus assured us that we can't serve two masters—money and God. We have to choose.

Once you choose to make God your Master, you can stop worrying about material needs. Jesus does not deny the legitimacy of our needs. He simply says they are not to be a significant focus of our devotion, energy, or pursuit. And above all, they should never be a cause of worry or fear. If these things do give rise to stress or anxiety, then we have reason to question whether God is truly our Master. We may be trying to serve two masters: God and money or material possessions.

*Step 6: Don't fear those who can only kill the body.* As we saw earlier, our first assignment in the pursuit of intimacy with God is to fear Him alone. Jesus knew His disciples would face tremendous persecution, yet they were not to fear any person. Today, most of us don't worry about being murdered. But how about other things that kill the body we inhabit? Every year, millions of people are diagnosed with potentially deadly diseases. After my son's cancer diagnosis, the words of Matthew 10:28 jumped off the page. God confirmed in my heart that the worst outcome of my son's cancer would be to kill his body. But that was not to be feared, because his soul was secure for eternity.

Jesus does not tell us to eliminate our emotions of fear but rather to live and act in spite of those emotions. We can't control our emotions, but we can control our choices and our behavior. When we embrace the fact that our earthly lives are temporary while our lives in Christ are eternal, our behavior starts to reflect that truth. The fears that once were debilitating are soon little more than momentary distractions. But it all starts with our faith in Him and acting on His commands and promises.

## ASSIGNMENT 5: LIVE IN THE PRESENT MOMENT

One of the greatest obstacles to living a life of faith is that our minds and hearts tend to focus on either the future or the past. The future could be ten minutes from now, and the past includes what happened five minutes ago. If we focus on either of these, we are not living in the moment. For example, if a colleague offends you and you are still affected by it when you arrive home that evening, you are not living in the moment. Or if you come home at six and you're distracted by concerns related to a meeting coming up the next morning, you are living in the future and won't be attentive to your family.

In Matthew 6:34, Jesus commanded, "Therefore do not worry about tomorrow, for tomorrow will worry about itself.

Each day has enough trouble of its own." Once again He began the statement with "therefore." So the basis for not worrying about tomorrow is the statement that immediately precedes it. "Your heavenly Father knows that you need them [food and drink and clothing]. But seek first his kingdom and his righteousness, and all these things will be given to you as well" (Matthew 6:32–33). We don't have to worry about or fear tomorrow because God will cover all our true needs when we pursue His Kingdom and righteousness.

But living in the future isn't the only distraction from pursuing God. We can be distracted by the past as well. It's easy to be mired in regret over past mistakes or in anger and hurt over a past offense. My dad would become so distressed about missed opportunities and past hurts that he often was consumed by bitterness. Jesus said, "No one who puts his hand to the plow and looks back is fit for service in the kingdom of God" (Luke 9:62).

If we are not to live in the future and we are not to look back, where does that put us? It puts us right where God wants us—in the moment! Only when we live in the moment can we be His representative to everyone He brings into our lives.

## ASSIGNMENT 6: OVERCOME TO THE END

Jesus never promised His followers easy lives. In fact, His call was, "If anyone would come after me, he must deny himself and take up his cross and follow me" (Matthew 16:24). There is nothing easy about dying to your own rights, needs, and desires. He told His disciples that they would be scattered, persecuted, and hated. But at the same time, He told them not to worry for He has overcome the world (John 16:33). And later, in His revelation to the apostle John, He gave the command to all His followers to "overcome." In fact, this is such an important calling that He gave twelve promises to those who would overcome:

1. They will receive the right to eat from the tree of life in paradise (Revelation 2:7).

2. They will not be hurt by the second death (Revelation 2:11).

3. Jesus will give them "hidden manna," supernatural nourishment (Revelation 2:17).

4. He will give each of them a "white stone with a new name written on it" (Revelation 2:17).

5. Jesus will give them "authority over the nations" (Revelation 2:26).

6. They will be clothed in white (Revelation 3:5).

7. Their names will never be erased from the book of life (Revelation 3:5).

8. Jesus will acknowledge their names before the Father and His angels (Revelation 3:5).

9. They will become pillars in the temple of God and will never have to leave it (Revelation 3:12).

10. Jesus will write the name of God and the name of the city of God upon them (Revelation 3:12).

11. Jesus will write upon them His new name (Revelation 3:12).

12. They will sit with Jesus on His throne (Revelation 3:21).

This raises the obvious question: What does Jesus mean when He tells us to "overcome"? Overcoming doesn't mean surviving or existing. It doesn't mean just getting by or marking time. It means being fully engaged in the calling of doing God's will right up to your final breath.

Overcoming is critical to our calling, and there are three ways to overcome by doing His will to the end. First, we must continually discover what Jesus said (His words, commands, and promises) and then obey what He said. Second, we must become committed and accountable to others in the body of Christ who also are committed to discovering and doing His will. Third, we must rely fully on the ministries of the Holy Spirit to continually lead us in our walk with Christ.

As we think about overcoming to the end, we come to the third of our four callings from Christ. This one moves from personal growth and spiritual maturity to reaching outward, beginning with fellow believers.

# THREE

# THE THIRD GIFT
# AND CALLING

*Empower Other Believers*

J esus commissioned His disciples to go throughout the world and preach the good news of God's gift of eternal life. Twenty centuries later, we should be no less dedicated to proclaiming the gospel. And yet, as important as it is to reach the unbelieving world, Jesus gave us another calling that is just as important. Jesus asked Peter three times, "Do you love me?" (John 21:15–17). Each time, when Peter answered yes, Jesus responded with commands that defined Peter's calling to minister to believers.

Specifically, Jesus told Peter to feed, nurture, lead, and take care of His sheep and lambs. Oh, how the Good Shepherd loves His sheep! And if this is how Peter was to demonstrate his love of the Savior, it also is a way we can express our love for Him. To this end, Jesus called us to accomplish three assignments that will help us empower other believers, a calling that is given along with the gift of God's promises to us.

## ASSIGNMENT 1: FEED
## AND SHEPHERD HIS SHEEP

The writer to the Hebrews said, "Without faith it is impossible to please God" (11:6). Paul wrote that "faith comes by hearing, and hearing by the word of God" (Romans 10:17, NKJV). In verse 14 he asked, "How shall they hear without a preacher?" (NKJV). In the Greek the word translated as "preacher" is a present-tense verb. It could more accurately be rendered as "one proclaiming." So the verse literally reads, "How shall they hear without someone proclaiming to them?" The first assignment of any believer in relation to other believers is to help them grow their faith by proclaiming the Word of God.

Yet proclaiming is only one of the assignments. The other is to shepherd, or take care of, Jesus's sheep. We do that by leading other Christians by our example. Sheep follow shepherds. We must walk the path that we want them to follow. The words that are used in John 21:15–17 to describe the concept of shepherding include the idea of tenderness. We are to tenderly take care of other believers. We should guide them with love and encouragement. Sheep are easily scared and scattered. Their lives and well-being depend on the nurture, care, and protection of a shepherd. Is this how you deal with your spouse, your children, and other believers you relate to?

### Action: Love One Another as He Has Loved Us

In John 13:34, Jesus revealed an action that is central to shepherding His sheep. "A new command I give you: Love one another. As I have loved you, so you must love one another." He repeated the command minutes later. "My command is this: Love each other as I have loved you. Greater love has no one than this, that he lay down his life for his friends. You are my friends if you do what I command" (John 15:12–14). The action that guides us in shepherding other believers is to love them the way Christ has loved us. That leads to two questions: How has He loved us, and how can we follow His example in loving the believers He brings into our lives?

Christ loves us in so many ways. He is light in our darkness, showing us the way we should go. He lived His life in righteousness for us, and He died for us. He tells us eternal truths, instructing us when His truth is contrary to our values, priorities, and lifestyles. He shows us tremendous patience, grace, and mercy. He is our best Friend and serves us in ways that we can't imagine. And though we are not capable of loving one another to that degree, we can love one another in the same manner.

## Action: Become Unified in Christ

In His final prayer before His arrest, Jesus told His Father,

> My prayer is not for them [His disciples] alone. I pray also for those who will believe in me through their message [that is, you and me], that all of them may be one, Father, just as you are in me and I am in you. May they also be in us so that the world may believe that you have sent me. I have given them the glory that you gave me, that they may be one as we are one: I in them and you in me. May they be brought to complete unity to let the world know that you sent me and have loved them even as you have loved me. (John 17:20–23)

How important is it to the Lord that we be unified with other believers? It's so important that as His crucifixion drew near and He had one last moment of prayer with the Father, He emphasized three times His desire that we be unified. Knowing that Jesus greatly desired it, shouldn't unity with other Christians become a major priority for each of us?

Christians hold conflicting doctrinal beliefs, and we never will be unified on all aspects of doctrine. The basis of our unity can be only one thing: the desire to discover and do what Jesus commanded. He said, "If anyone would come after me, he must deny himself and take up his cross and follow me" (Matthew 16:24). That verse contains the secret to unity. If the focus of your life is to deny yourself, take up your cross, and follow Jesus, then you can have unity with any believer who wants those same things. The more closely we follow Christ, the closer we grow in unity with others.

The problem is that most American Christians make their Christianity about everything but following Christ. Sound doctrine is important. But it was never meant to be our primary focus. Following Christ was always meant to be our chief focus. As we dedicate ourselves to following Jesus by discovering and doing what He commands, we move closer to Him. And the closer we move toward Christ, the closer we move toward unity with one another.

To this end, a growing number of Christians, churches, and organizations are working to encourage churches and individual believers to begin to focus on discovering the teachings of Christ and applying them to every area of life.[1]

## ASSIGNMENT 2: STRENGTHEN YOUR BROTHERS AND SISTERS

At the Last Supper, Jesus told Peter that Satan would sift him like wheat (Luke 22:31). But Jesus also told him, "I have prayed for you, Simon, that your faith may not fail." Then He gave Peter an assignment that he was to focus on after repenting: "And *when* you have turned back, strengthen your brothers" (verse 32). Knowing the Good Shepherd's love of His sheep, we can safely assume that He would have us engage in this assignment with the same commitment He was demanding of Peter.

So the question is, how can we strengthen other believers? Jesus tells us to love one another in the same manner that He has loved us. He loves us by giving us His Word to guide us; listening to our hearts—our joys and our sorrows; extending us an ear when we need to be heard; giving us comfort; giving us encouragement; and nurturing us in our relationship with Him. We can strengthen one another by doing these same things. And last but not least, we can pray for one another.

## ASSIGNMENT 3: TEACH OTHERS TO OBSERVE EVERYTHING CHRIST COMMANDED

For a number of years, I was involved with an evangelical organization in which adherents frequently quoted the Great Commission—but only part of it. We quoted Matthew 28:19: "Go ye therefore, and teach all nations, baptizing them in the name of the Father, and of the Son, and of the Holy Ghost" (KJV). But we overlooked Jesus's focal point: "and teaching them to obey everything I have commanded you" (verse 20).

To skip verse 20 is to end the statement midsentence. If you read the end of Matthew 28 without the verse numbers, it says, "Therefore go and make disciples of all nations, baptizing them in the name of the Father and of the Son and of the Holy Spirit, and teaching them to obey everything I have commanded you." Christ told us to make disciples by teaching believers to obey His commands and teachings.

It is impossible to overstate the importance of Jesus's teachings and commands. Obeying what He said is not only the way we express our love for Him, but it also is the way we must live as disciples. Further, it is the way we lead other believers into discipleship. Obedience to Christ is central to our relationship with Him. If you do the will of the Father, Jesus calls you His brother, sister, and mother (Matthew 12:50).

Now we come to the last of our four callings from Christ. He calls us to invest in the lives of nonbelievers.

# FOUR

# THE FOURTH GIFT
# AND CALLING

*Impact the Lives
of Nonbelievers*

Can you remember who introduced you to the reality and truth of the Person of Jesus Christ? What was your initial response? How long did it take from the time you first heard about Christ until you made a full commitment to follow Him?

How many other people had a positive effect on your attitude toward Christ prior to your making a commitment? What would your life be like today had they never reached out to you? For the Christians who spoke to you about Christ, you were a white field ready for harvest.

Sharing the reality of Jesus Christ with nonbelievers is not just an option; it is a calling. And along with this calling, Jesus gave us specific assignments as well as the gift of His presence and the power of His Spirit as we reach out to nonbelievers.

## ASSIGNMENT 1: REACH OUT NOW

It is easy to miss the opportunity of the moment because we are thinking about the near past or the near future. At work, we may walk past the receptionist without saying a word because we're thinking about a meeting that's coming up, or an argument we had with our spouse the night before. Our natural inclination is to let our focus remain on ourselves and our circumstances. In John 4:35, Jesus said, "Do you not say, 'There are still four months and then comes the harvest'? Behold, I say to you, lift up your eyes and look at the fields, for they are already white for harvest!" (NKJV).

Jesus tells us to stop procrastinating. The fields are already white for harvest. When I walk into work, every person God brings into my path will be my "white field" at that moment. We are to be Jesus's representative to whomever He puts before us.

When I board an airplane tomorrow, my white field will be the flight attendants, the passenger in the seat next to me, and others. Does this mean I preach to everyone? Not at all. But it does mean that if someone needs to talk, I become the compassionate ears of Christ. If someone needs a hug, I become the arms of Christ. If someone needs encouragement, I become Christ's giver of hope and encouragement. And if someone needs to hear the gospel, I share Christ.

Jesus commanded this, and He demonstrated it. Because of His encounter with the woman at the well, an entire village was evangelized. Jesus started out by focusing on a woman who was His white field at that moment. How many white fields will you encounter in the next twenty-four hours? Will you be caught looking down, or will you reap the harvest? Undertaking this assignment has the power to turn every day into a tremendous series of blessings for you and for those you encounter.

## ASSIGNMENT 2: OPEN YOUR EYES TO THE WHITE FIELDS

Every morning when you wake up, tell the Lord that today you are on a mission for Him. Then ask Him to open your eyes to every white field. Ask the Holy Spirit to make you sensitive to His promptings. Realize that you have the power to express the love of Christ in different ways, whether it's giving someone a smile and a greeting, or encouraging him or her with a word, or applying God's Word to a situation that person is going through.

## ASSIGNMENT 3: GET INVOLVED IN SOWING AND REAPING

After Jesus told His disciples to lift up their eyes and look at the fields, He said,

> And he who reaps receives wages, and gathers fruit for eternal life, that both he who sows and he who reaps may rejoice together. For in this the saying is true: "One sows and another reaps." I sent you to reap that for which you have not labored; others have labored, and you have entered into their labors. (John 4:36–38, NKJV)

We sow the gospel by spreading God's Word like seeds into the minds of others. You might share Jesus's words from

Matthew 11:28–29 with a person in the midst of adversity or deep sorrow: "Come to me, all you who are weary and burdened, and I will give you rest. Take my yoke upon you and learn from me, for I am gentle and humble in heart, and you will find rest for your souls." I often incorporate God's Word into conversations and seminars that I teach. I have taught executives of Fortune 500 companies a seminar about achieving extraordinary outcomes. Two of the strategies are effective partnering and a process called vision mapping. When I talk about partnering, I quote Proverbs 15:22, "Plans fail for lack of counsel, but with many advisers they succeed," and Proverbs 11:14 (NKJV), "Where there is no counsel, the people fall; but in the multitude of counselors there is safety." When I talk about vision mapping, I quote Proverbs 29:18 (KJV), "Where there is no vision, the people perish." Sowing seeds can be as simple as that.

On the reaping side, I have had the joy of seeing many people commit their lives to following Jesus. Remember that it is never your job to try to persuade people to commit their lives to Christ. You simply share your testimony and God's Word. It is the Holy Spirit's responsibility to draw them into God's Kingdom.

## ASSIGNMENT 4: BEAR FRUIT

In His conversation with the disciples at the Last Supper, Jesus revealed one of the most important callings of a disciple. Because of the black-and-white nature of His statements, we must see this as an assignment given to all of us.

Jesus compared His disciples (and us) to the branches of a grapevine and compared Himself to the trunk of the vine. He compared God the Father to the Gardener who cares for the vine. Later, Christ revealed that His words are the life-giving sap that enables the branches to bear fruit. In this analogy He revealed seven truths that must have been startling to His disciples (John 15:1–8).

1. The purpose of the Vine and its branches is to bear much fruit (verse 2).

2. Healthy branches (followers of Christ) bear a lot of fruit (verse 5).

3. The life-giving, fruit-producing sap in the branches comes from the Vine (Christ) (verses 4–5).

4. If the branch doesn't remain in a healthy relationship with the Vine, it cannot bear fruit (verses 5–6).

5. If the branch does remain in a healthy relationship with the Vine, it will bear much fruit (verse 5).

6. If the branch does not bear fruit, then it is cut off and thrown away (verse 6).

7. If the branch bears fruit, it is pruned so it can bear even more (verse 2).

Jesus reveals two additional truths. First, His spoken word makes us clean (verse 3). Second, if we abide (dwell or remain) in Him and His words abide (dwell or remain) in us, then we can ask whatever we wish, and it will be given to us—and we will bear much fruit (verses 7–8). Amazing! He promises that when we meditate on His words and do them, His words will make us clean. Further, His words will become the master key to receiving what we pray for and to our bearing much fruit.

## ASSIGNMENT 5: BE HIS WITNESS

Jesus's last statement to His followers before He ascended into heaven is recorded in Acts 1:8: "You will receive power when the Holy Spirit comes on you; and you will be my witnesses in Jerusalem, and in all Judea and Samaria, and to the ends of the earth." The assignment is to publicly and privately testify of Jesus, His work, and His words. The two initial actions for the apostles related to this assignment were (1) to wait until the Holy Spirit came upon them and infused them with power and then (2) to be His witnesses, starting in Jerusalem, then to Judea, then to Samaria, and ultimately to the entire world.

What do these actions mean for us? First, it is the Holy Spirit who empowers us to be effective witnesses for Christ. Second, our witness should start wherever we spend the most time—at home, at the office, in our community—and then extend outward into every place and culture where the Lord calls us.

## Action: Declare Jesus Openly

In Matthew 10:32–33, Jesus told His disciples, "Therefore whoever confesses Me before men, him I will also confess before My Father who is in heaven. But whoever denies Me before men, him I will also deny before My Father who is in heaven" (NKJV). The word translated "confess" could also be translated "openly declare" or "freely speak." So Jesus's statement could be rendered as "Therefore whoever openly declares Me before men, him I will also openly declare before My Father." Do you have any trouble talking to others about your spouse or your kids? Probably not. After all, they are an inseparable part of who you are. So why should talking about Jesus be any different? If you have been born again, He is not only your Savior but also your most important family member. The apostle Peter said it like this: "In your hearts set apart Christ as Lord. Always be prepared to give an answer to everyone who asks you to give the reason for the hope that you have. But do this with gentleness and respect" (1 Peter 3:15).

We are to be real and transparent with others concerning our relationship with Christ. We are to give Him credit for what He has done in our lives. And we are not to be aggressive, arrogant, or condescending in the way we share the gospel.

## ASSIGNMENT 6: GO OUT AND PREACH THE GOSPEL TO EVERYONE

Jesus gave His final exhortation shortly before He ascended into heaven. Mark wrote, "He said to them, 'Go into all the world and preach the good news to all creation'" (16:15). It could be argued that this was a specific command and calling intended only for His original disciples. However, even if that were true, we could view the principle behind the command and embrace the assignment. The Greek word that is translated "preach" (*kēryssō*) can be rendered as "to formally and powerfully proclaim (as a herald)." It also can mean "to proclaim openly something that has happened." With that understanding, preaching the gospel can apply to any of us.

I have had the joy of proclaiming the realities of Jesus in countless situations—to audiences as small as one person and as large as a full arena. Whether your audience is one, ten, or ten thousand, the more intimate you become with the Lord, the more freely you will be able to preach the gospel. And as we saw earlier, our goal is not simply to preach salvation but, equally important, to lead people into discipleship by "teaching them to obey everything I [Jesus] have commanded you" (Matthew 28:20).

## ASSIGNMENT 7: PREACH REPENTANCE AND FORGIVENESS OF SINS

Today you can hear sermons and read Christian books that will tell you almost everything about any topic of interest.

But they don't always match the emphasis we see in Jesus's teachings. I've heard people share messages with themes such as "Come to Jesus and have a happier marriage, a more successful career, a happier life!" Although such themes may reflect the speaker's personal experience, you won't find Jesus making such offers. Not only is Jesus the "author and finisher of our faith" (Hebrews 12:2, NKJV), but He should also be the Author and Finisher of our message.

In Luke 24:46–47, Jesus told His disciples, "This is what is written: The Christ will suffer and rise from the dead on the third day, and repentance and forgiveness of sins will be preached in his name to all nations, beginning at Jerusalem." Thus, the focus of our outreach to nonbelievers must be announcing the need for repentance and the good news that forgiveness of sins is available to any who would believe the gospel and follow Christ.

However, for such a message to be relevant, listeners must first have a clear understanding of where they stand before God. They first need to realize that God is perfect in His righteousness, and they are lost in their sins. Only then can they know that they need forgiveness and need to repent from their sin (Romans 3:23; 6:23). In Ephesians 2 (NKJV),

Paul wrote that we were "dead…in sins" (verse 1) and had "no hope" (verse 12). Dead is dead, without any opportunity for life. And "no hope" means none whatsoever!

But that's not the end. "But God, who is rich in mercy, because of His great love with which He loved us, even when we were dead in trespasses, made us alive together with Christ" (verses 4–5, NKJV). To effectively share the message, we must communicate the reason that repentance and forgiveness are needed.

## ASSIGNMENT 8: SPEAK IN THE DAYLIGHT WHAT CHRIST TOLD YOU AT NIGHT

In Matthew 10, as Jesus prepared to send His disciples out to preach, He gave them a number of instructions. Then, almost out of the blue, He told them, "What I tell you in the dark, speak in the daylight; what is whispered in your ear, proclaim from the roofs" (verse 27). Although this was a specific command given to the twelve apostles, it reveals a wonderful command and activity for us as well. For most believers, the best time to meditate on the words of Jesus is at night. I usually spend time reading His words on a topic from the Gospels. Without fail, He talks to me through His words on the page, and I engage in a quiet two-way conversation about what He's saying to me. And because I take this assignment seriously, I often tell my wife, children, or others what Jesus revealed the night before. Whenever I do this, I see His words and revelation bless the hearts and minds of others.

Throughout the day I often hear the Holy Spirit whisper Jesus's words to me. This is one of the eleven ministries of the Holy Spirit that Jesus revealed in the gospel of John. In John 14:26, Jesus said, "The Helper, the Holy Spirit, whom the Father will send in My name, He will teach you all things, and bring to your remembrance all things that I said to you" (NKJV). Sometimes His whispers are meant only for me and a particular choice I am facing. Sometimes they are meant for me to quietly share with just one person, and sometimes they are meant for me to openly proclaim in a group setting. When He reveals a treasure to you from His Word, more often than not it's not just for you; it's for the people He brings into your path as well. What He speaks to you at night, share in the daylight.

## ASSIGNMENT 9: BE THE SALT OF THE EARTH

In the Sermon on the Mount, Jesus called His disciples "the salt of the earth" (Matthew 5:13). At the time of Christ, salt provided the only means of preserving food. Trade routes used for transporting salt were called salt roads. In America during the War of 1812, soldiers were paid with salt brine instead of money. When Jesus called His disciples "the salt of the earth," He was telling them they were of extreme worth to Him and of critical importance to the world. They were to preserve the truth about Jesus and His teachings and consequently become the preserving and purifying influence in the world.

He went on to say, "But if the salt loses its saltiness, how can it be made salty again? It is no longer good for anything, except to be thrown out and trampled by men" (verse 13). In other words, if the day ever came that Christ's disciples no longer embraced and proclaimed the truths of the gospel, they would no longer have a preserving or purifying influence. The rotting and spoilage of the world would quickly follow.

We can become the salt of the earth as we discover and follow the teachings of Christ. Our lives can become salt, conveying His love and righteousness and their preserving power to those around us.

## ASSIGNMENT 10: BE THE LIGHT OF THE WORLD

In John 8:12, Jesus said, "I am the light of the world. Whoever follows me will never walk in darkness, but will have the light of life." Without the revelation of the Person of Christ and the Word of God, we would live in a world of spiritual darkness. We would be in danger of accepting all the world's standards and values as truth. But Jesus is the Light of the world, and His words reveal truth about ourselves, about God, and about what He values, loves, and hates. As we walk in the path He walked before us, we won't have to stumble and fall in the darkness.

Immediately after Jesus called His disciples the "salt of the earth," He called them the "light of the world" (Matthew 5:14)—but in a very different context than the statement He made about Himself ( John 8:12). He provides light so

His followers won't have to walk in darkness. With His light showing us the Truth, we can walk in the paths of love and righteousness that He walked.

As His disciples, we are commissioned to be lights of "good deeds." Jesus said, "You are the light of the world. A city on a hill cannot be hidden. Neither do people light a lamp and put it under a bowl. Instead they put it on its stand, and it gives light to everyone in the house. In the same way, let your light shine before men, that they may see your good deeds and praise your Father in heaven" (Matthew 5:14–16).

My best friends apart from my wife and children are Jim Shaughnessy and Gary Smalley. For forty years, Jim has been a light for my world. Anytime I wonder how to let Jesus's love flow through me, I need only to think of Jim. And when it comes to dealing with adversity or trials, I need only think of the times when I've seen Gary Smalley respond to adversity. That is what Jesus called you and me to be and do. Our words are critically important in reaching and blessing others, but they are not nearly as important as the light we provide by doing acts of love and righteousness that reflect the light of God's Son.

# FIVE

# ROADBLOCKS AND BOOBY TRAPS

*Be Aware of the Deadly Detours*
*to Following Christ*

E ven though we have a clear calling from Christ on how to follow Him and experience a growing intimacy with God, doing so does not come naturally. Following Christ is contrary to our nature. In Matthew 7:21–23 we see Jesus declare to many of His professed followers that He *never knew them.* And even though they had prophesied, cast out demons, and performed miracles in His name, He banned them from His presence. In the second and third chapters of Revelation, we read His striking reproofs to six churches and we see how whole churches and their members had lost their love for Christ and were no longer following Him in the ways that He had commanded. His startling words to the Laodiceans in Revelation 3:14–22 seem to be descriptive of many professing Christians who fill countless American churches. The same confounding obstacles and deadly traps that Jesus warned His first-century followers about are the ones that keep so many of today's evangelicals from truly following Him.

Can a sovereign God remove these obstacles? Absolutely! But it's important to recognize what they are. The most common traps frequently go unnoticed. And for many, when they are seen, they often seem harmless. Yet they can have a deadly outcome.

There is a second reason we need to be aware of the traps. They not only stand between people and the second birth, but they can keep those who are already born again from becoming more intimate with God and from fulfilling the callings that Jesus gave His followers. The traps can prevent us from receiving the promised gifts that accompany our callings from Christ.

Six obstacles stand out as the most common roadblocks. Heading the list is pride, by far the greatest obstacle that blinds people to the Kingdom and callings of God.

## OBSTACLE 1: PRIDE

During a 1957 evangelistic crusade in New York City, Billy Graham proclaimed that nothing keeps more people out of

God's Kingdom than pride. It is deadly to nonbelievers, blinding them to a vision of God and His truth. Pride also inflicts damage on believers, preventing an intimate relationship with God.

When the Pharisees grilled the young man whose blindness Jesus healed, their pride and self-righteousness were obvious. They said, "You were steeped in sin at birth; how dare you lecture us!" (John 9:34), implying that they were not born in sin. They believed they were far more righteous than the formerly blind man.

Pride and self-righteousness blind us to reality, to the Lord, and to His commands and promises. Pride can keep us living in darkness even when we think we are living in the light. Jesus said, "I tell you the truth, unless you change and become like little children, you will never enter the kingdom of heaven. Therefore, whoever humbles himself like this child is the greatest in the kingdom of heaven" (Matthew 18:3–4). Children are dependent on others to meet their needs. The reason we must become like children is that we must see we are spiritually bankrupt. On our own, we have no resources to remedy our spiritual inadequacy. So we must exercise faith, take God at His word, and become totally dependent on Him.

The basis of genuine humility is seeing ourselves as God sees us and seeing Him as He really is. When those visions become our reality, we become aware that all that we have is because of God's grace and what He and others have given to us (1 Corinthians 4:7). Peter told us, "God resists the proud, but gives grace to the humble" (1 Peter 5:5, NKJV). If it's grace that you want, then pay heed to what Peter said next: "Therefore humble yourselves under the mighty hand of God, that He may exalt you in due time" (verse 6, NKJV).

## OBSTACLE 2: SELF-RIGHTEOUSNESS

If pride is the number-one obstacle to coming to know God and His grace, then self-righteousness is a close second. All of us can find merit in our own behavior. We can always find someone whose life is "less righteous" than ours, which gives us a false sense of goodness. "I may not be Mother Teresa, but I'm basically a good person. In fact, I'm a lot better than my friend at work."

The Gallup organization stated that 81 percent of Americans believe in heaven.[2] And if the survey had asked, the researchers would have found that most of those people also think they are going to heaven. They are comfortable with where they are in relation to good and evil, God and the devil, heaven and hell.

For most people a mistaken belief in their own righteousness rests on four deadly errors in judgment. First, they misjudge who God is and how He acts. Second, they misjudge themselves, minimizing the reality of their sin and its deadly consequences. Third, they don't understand that God has provided only one way for sinners (which includes all of us) to get into heaven. And finally, they don't understand who Jesus is, what He said, what He offers, and what He demands of us.

These four errors in judgment feed self-righteousness, preventing people from trusting God.

## 1. Misjudgments About Who God Is and How He Acts

*Error:* Because God loves us, He won't condemn anyone except people who are really bad.

*Truth:* God does not conform to our hopes or preferences. He defines His own nature and character, and His dealings with humanity emanate from His nature. It is impossible for God to violate His character.

God defines Himself by three attributes: His kindness, His justice or judgment, and His righteousness (Jeremiah 9:24). None of these can cancel out or violate the others. God hates sin and loves righteousness. His justice requires that He punish sin and reward righteousness. His love causes Him to extend His grace and mercy to unrighteous humanity. In light of our sin and God's unchangeable character, the only way He can extend His grace and mercy to us is to do it in a way that does not violate His righteousness and justice.

There was only one just and righteous solution to our sin—a substitute who would receive all the punishment that we deserve. But that substitute would have to be Someone who had never sinned; this had to be a perfect sacrifice. The only way for this to happen was for God to send His Son to earth to make the sacrifice.

## 2. Misjudgments About Our Own Goodness

*Error:* I am basically a good person, and I know a lot of people who are a lot worse.

*Truth:* Have you ever been angry? Have you ever been envious? Have you ever had a lustful thought about someone other than your spouse? If your answer is yes, you fall woefully short of God's standard for goodness.

God sets the standard for goodness, and no human has ever made the grade. Have you ever had a day when you failed to love God with all your heart, mind, soul, and strength? Have you ever failed to love your neighbor in the same way you love yourself? If you are guilty of any of these things, you are guilty of violating God's moral laws. And His righteousness and justice demand that you die spiritually. According to Jesus, you and I and everyone else have broken God's greatest laws and must pay the eternal consequences. God said that even our best actions are like filthy rags compared to His perfect righteousness (Isaiah 64:6).

God compares our values, words, actions, behavior, thoughts, and motives to His perfect righteousness, and by that standard we fall infinitely short. Without the atoning sacrifice of Jesus Christ, we would have no hope of making it into heaven.

*3. Errors of Judgment Regarding God's Path to Heaven*
*Error:* There are many paths to heaven, and if we try to do our best, we will be on a path that leads to eternal life.

*Truth:* Jesus said, "I am *the* way, *the* truth, and *the* life. No one comes to the Father except through Me" (John 14:6, NKJV).

Only two paths are available, and they lead to opposite destinations. "Enter through the narrow gate," Jesus said. "For wide is the gate and broad is the road that leads to destruction, and many enter through it. But small is the gate and narrow the road that leads to life, and only a few find it" (Matthew 7:13–14). People who follow the wide path to destruction will spend eternity separated from God, but those who find the narrow path will spend eternity with God. The wide path is a crowded road, because it's the one that most people take. The second road is more like a narrow footpath, able to accommodate people only if they walk in single file. Most people don't choose that path.

The narrow path is a life of following Jesus, discovering what He said and doing it. He restated the contrast of the two paths by using a second analogy. There are two foundations on which you can build your life: one is rock; the other is sand. Lives built on the rock will be secure, and those people will enter heaven. Lives built on sand will collapse, and those people will spend eternity cut off from God. Jesus said the foundation of rock is hearing His words and doing them, and the unstable foundation of sand is hearing His words and *not* doing them (Matthew 7:24–27).

## 4. Errors in Judgment Regarding Who Jesus Is, What He Said, What He Offers, and What He Demands

*Error:* Jesus was a Gandhi-like or Mother Teresa–like figure who walked around teaching about peace and alleviating human suffering. He offers heaven to everyone and demands nothing in return.

*Truth:* Jesus came to earth to accomplish twenty-seven missions. He made more than nineteen hundred statements that are recorded, which we can study and live by. He came to reveal the truth about God the Father, Himself, eternal life, and His Kingdom.

He lived a sinless life and sacrificed Himself as the full payment for the sins of all who would place their faith in Him. This faith is evidenced by a life of discovering and following Jesus's teachings and commands. He offers no hope to anyone who doesn't follow Him. Like the Father, Jesus is a God of righteousness and justice as well as a God of love.

## OBSTACLE 3: RELIGIOUS ACTIVITY
## AND TRADITION

How could the most religious people on the planet miss their own Messiah? The Pharisees met a formerly blind man who had been healed by Jesus. They heard about hundreds of other miracles, things that had never been seen before. Jesus was fulfilling dozens of prophecies from the Pharisees' most sacred scriptures. But did they choose to sit at the feet of this miracle-working Rabbi and feast on His teachings? No, they attacked Him because He violated their traditions! It sounds like insanity, but it is a prime example of the blinding power of religion. Their man-made traditions blinded them to the presence of their Messiah!

The Pharisees studied the Scriptures for hours every day. They were careful to obey the letter of the Law, including hundreds of Israel's civil, social, and ceremonial laws. And yet their devotion to religious activity blinded them to the truth. Jesus referred to them as the blind leading the blind (Matthew 15:14) and as "whitewashed tombs,…beautiful on the outside but…full of…everything unclean" (Matthew 23:27).

Jesus told them, "You diligently study the Scriptures because you think that by them you possess eternal life" (John 5:39). Jesus repeatedly called them hypocrites, and in Luke 16:15, He summed it up with "You are the ones who justify yourselves in the eyes of men, but God knows your hearts. What is highly valued among men is detestable in God's sight."

Today, Christians have given priority to studying subjects such as the gifts of the Holy Spirit, prophecy, the rapture, prosperity and health, or social justice—all to the neglect of the teachings and callings of the Lord Jesus. We have done the very thing that Jesus lambasted the Pharisees for doing. Countless professing Christians have a "form of godliness" (2 Timothy 3:5), but their lives are void of the power of the gospel. While many want a more intimate relationship with God, few seem to know how to achieve it. And even the most sincere believers today are less knowledgeable of the statements of Jesus than any generation of believers since the Reformation.

I'm not opposed to Christians learning about prophecy or any other subject taught in the Bible. But no activity and no single subject should be allowed to overshadow the goal of gaining an intimate relationship with God, a level of intimacy that comes only by following the teachings of Jesus.

Jesus summed up His call in Matthew 16:24: "If anyone desires to come after Me, let him deny himself, and take up his cross, and follow Me" (NKJV). The only way we can follow Him is to discover His words and do them. We follow His words by faith, empowered by God's grace. Jesus's promises and commands are the only secure foundation upon which true faith can rest. And yet most Christians spend little time meditating on either Christ's promises or His commands. The Bread of Life is tasted by many but consumed by few. Many church members are starving spiritually.[3]

The most devastating consequence of religious distractions is that they provide a false sense of security, which will be shattered for many professing believers when they come face to face with Christ (Matthew 7:13–23).[4]

## OBSTACLE 4: WEALTH

One day a young man knelt in front of Jesus and asked, "What good thing shall I do that I may have eternal life?"

(Matthew 19:16, NKJV). When Jesus told him to keep the commandments, the man asked, "Which ones?" (verse 18). Jesus named six commandments, including "You shall love your neighbor as yourself" (verse 19, NKJV). The young man confidently replied that he had kept all of these. He then asked, "What do I still lack?" (verse 20). Amazingly, this man had a chance to have the most important question of his life answered by the *only* One who could answer it authoritatively.

Jesus wanted this young man to receive eternal life. At the same time, Jesus could not compromise the truth. Jesus told the man, "Sell your possessions and give to the poor, and you will have treasure in heaven. Then come, follow me" (verse 21).

How could Jesus make such a terrible demand? The answer is simple. Like everyone else, this man could enter the Kingdom of God only by being born again. The evidence of such a new birth would be the opening of the man's eyes to his sin and to the surpassing greatness of Christ. His heart would turn to repentance, and the man would do an about-face from his self-centered hoarding of wealth. He would joyfully follow the only One who could give him eternal life.

A command from Jesus to sell everything and follow Him would be easy to follow for a person who had been born again. However, it would not be doable for anyone who sought eternal life on his own terms. This man's wealth was his god, in violation of the first of the Ten Commandments (Exodus 20:3). And yet he foolishly believed he had kept all of God's commandments. His resistance to giving away his wealth showed that he also had lived in violation of the second greatest command: "You shall love your neighbor as yourself" (Mark 12:31, NKJV).

Jesus had made the most incredible offer of all time! But the man refused Jesus's offer because only a person who is born again would gladly trade his temporary possessions for eternal life. The young man walked away. Then Jesus said to His disciples, "I tell you the truth, it is hard for a rich man to enter the kingdom of heaven. Again I tell you, it is easier for a camel to go through the eye of a needle than for a rich man to enter the kingdom of God" (Matthew 19:23–24). The disciples exclaimed, "Who then can be saved?" Jesus replied, "With man this is impossible, but with God all things are possible" (verses 25–26).

Why is it so hard for the rich to enter God's Kingdom?

Because wealth breeds arrogance, a spirit of independence, and a desire to be served by others. But to follow Christ, we must desire the exact opposite. We must humble ourselves, become dependent on Him, and desire to serve God and others instead of being served.

It is humanly impossible to overcome the obstacle of wealth to get into the Kingdom of God. But when God gives the second birth to a person, regardless of his or her wealth (or lack of it), the impossible is accomplished—but only by God. This is great news for all of us in America since most Americans are far richer than the vast majority of the world's population. So we all are like camels trying to pass through the eye of a needle. We can't do it unless we are truly born again.

## OBSTACLE 5: MISPLACED VALUES

On July 16, 1999, John F. Kennedy Jr., his wife, Carolyn, and her sister Lauren climbed into a single-engine plane to fly from New Jersey to Martha's Vineyard in Massachusetts. John was still a rookie pilot, having received his pilot's license only fifteen months earlier. His wife didn't like flying with him on private planes because she didn't feel he had been flying long enough. This time, reportedly, they had disagreed over whether to fly commercial or private to a family wedding celebration. She gave in.

Once John arrived at the airport, he got the report that haze blanketed the New England coast. At that same New Jersey airport, another private pilot with much more experience heard the report and decided not to fly. John did not have an instrument rating or the training to fly in low visibility. He didn't worry about it, however, because he failed to recognize the degree of danger. He knew about vertigo, a condition that can develop when visibility is bad. But he didn't think it would be a problem. Besides, he wanted to get to the party sooner than a commercial airline could get him there.

Later that night he did get vertigo. He had no idea that his plane's nose was pointed down, toward the waters of the Atlantic. Because he had no idea how to read the instruments, he was disoriented. He wasn't able to straighten out the aircraft. His plane continued to accelerate until it crashed. He, his wife, and her sister were killed.

How could this happen to such an intelligent man? Simply stated, he placed a high value on what wasn't that important and no value on what was critically important. He placed a high value on getting to a party early and the ego satisfaction of flying there himself. He placed no value on his wife's concerns, no value on the weather conditions, and no value on what he had learned about the dangers of not being able to identify the horizon in hazy conditions. His misplaced values cost three lives.

By the time most of us are confronted with the gospel, the values of the world have been deeply ingrained into our nature. We saw this in the story of the rich young ruler. He valued his possessions and his comfortable life, and those values were so ingrained that he couldn't break free. On the other hand, other wealthy people encountered Jesus, and because they were born again, they were able to break free of the world's values to embrace God's values.

Zacchaeus was a chief tax collector. That meant he was rich largely because he was a cheat. Rome allowed him to keep a certain percentage of the taxes he collected. So in order to collect more, he often assessed higher taxes on people than they really owed. He kept not only his rightful percentage of the honest collection of taxes but also 100 percent of the overcharges.

One day when Jesus was passing through Jericho, the crowd around Him was so dense that Zacchaeus ran ahead and climbed a tree so he could see Jesus. As Jesus walked past, He looked into the tree and said, "Zacchaeus, come down immediately. I must stay at your house today" (Luke 19:5). At his home Zacchaeus told the Lord he had decided to give half of his possessions to the poor and to pay back every person he cheated, at the rate of four times the amount he had taken.

Unlike the rich young ruler, Zacchaeus transformed his values. He valued his relationship with Jesus far more than he valued his money or possessions. For all we know, paying back everyone four times the amount he had cheated them may have bankrupted him. But he didn't take time to calculate his losses; he made the commitment to do what was right.

Previously, Jesus had said it was easier for a camel to pass through the eye of a needle than for a rich man to enter the Kingdom of God. But to Zacchaeus, our Savior said, "Today salvation has come to this house, because he also is a son of

Abraham; for the Son of Man has come to seek and to save that which was lost" (Luke 19:9–10, NKJV). A rich man had been born again, and Jesus saw the evidence of that new birth in Zacchaeus's heart, spirit, and behavior.

What do you value more than you should, and what do you fail to value as much as you should? The truth is, when we are born again and begin to have an intimate relationship with God, our values begin changing to Christ's values. When we follow Christ, we discover what He said and we start doing it. Missionary Jim Elliot followed Christ all the way into the jungles of Ecuador, taking the gospel to the most feared tribe in South America. It cost him his life at age twenty-nine. But before he was martyred, he said, "He is no fool who gives what he cannot keep to gain what he cannot lose."[5] Jim Elliot was no fool. Like Zacchaeus, his treasures in heaven are great.

## OBSTACLE 6: PROCRASTINATION

Millions of people say they want a closer relationship with God. And yet year after year they continue doing what they've always done.

Yesterday I boarded a plane for home and sat next to a young man traveling to a business meeting. He was thirty-four years old and married, with two children. He said something that hinted that he was a believer, so I asked how long he had been a Christian. He said he had "accepted Christ" at a young age, then lost all interest when he was in college. He fell in love with a girl he later married. One day she said, "When are we going to start attending church?" Soon they got involved in an evangelical church, and his wife committed her life to Christ. He recommitted his life to Christ as well.

But as we talked about what real intimacy with God entails, he said he was so immersed in his work and other things that he kept putting it off. However, he hoped things would change in the future. That's when I asked him a question that seemed to rattle him: "How would you feel if your children came face to face with Jesus Christ, and He told them, 'I never knew you'? Imagine if they replied, 'But Dad said that if I prayed to receive You, I would go to heaven.' And they heard Christ say again, 'I never knew you. Depart from Me!'

"You say you want to work on your relationship with

God, but you keep putting it off. And instead of seeing a dad who has a thriving, intimate walk with God, your children see a dad who talks about Jesus instead of following Him. How long are you going to wait before you decide to pursue a truly intimate relationship with God?"

Already, he had lost ten years of experiencing the joy that Jesus longs to give (John 15:10–11). Ten years of setting a godly example for his wife, his children, and all who closely observe his life.

Have you been procrastinating in the area of being born again or moving into greater intimacy with Christ? God is not obligated to continue extending His grace to those who ignore it. In Luke 13:5, Jesus said, "Unless you repent, you too will all perish." He then told a parable in verses 6 through 9 that implied that God will put up with those who procrastinate for only so long. When we procrastinate, we are telling Him that our desires and values are more important than His. That shows that pride controls our lives, and God has promised to resist the proud but give grace to the humble (1 Peter 5:5).

Procrastination is an invisible fence between you and God. It's so much a part of our nature that we are unaware of it. We intend to do what is right as soon as we have time. But we deceive ourselves into thinking that we don't have time right now. We may fool ourselves, but we don't fool God. Stop procrastinating and start obeying His words now, while He is extending His grace to you.

And now, this question must be considered: How about *you*? What obstacles are keeping you from embracing and pursuing our Savior's callings to you? Each calling is real. Each calling is transformational. And if you respond to each one, not only will you "bear much fruit," but you will forever change the lives of those whom God brings into your life daily.

# SIX

# PROMISES YOU CAN BUILD YOUR FAITH ON

*We Love Jesus by Obeying Him,
and He Promises All the Help
We'll Ever Need*

Christ's promises are a gift. They provide a foundation that will withstand the greatest storms that life can throw at you. Jesus made more than one hundred promises to His followers.[6] Most are conditional promises, in which Jesus set a condition that if a person obeys a particular command, then Jesus assures a promised outcome. For example, in John 6:40 He said, "Everyone who looks to the Son and believes in him shall have eternal life, and I will raise him up at the last day." The promises here are twofold: eternal life and to be raised up by Christ on the last day. The condition is that you look to the Son and believe in Him.[7]

The conditional promises Jesus made to you offer benefits that include eternal life, escape from eternal judgment, becoming a member of His family, intimacy with God, the ultimate in joy and peace, experiencing miracles, being cleansed from sin, and seeing your life produce eternal "fruit." And these are just a few of the riches He promises.

If we were to group Jesus's promises, they would fall into more than twenty-four categories. In this chapter I have listed a few of the promises to help you see how Christ's promises apply to your life.

## PROMISES ABOUT ETERNAL LIFE

Most assuredly, I say to you, he who hears My word and believes in Him who sent Me has everlasting life, and shall not come into judgment, but has passed from death into life. (John 5:24, NKJV)

I am the resurrection and the life. He who believes in me will live, even though he dies. (John 11:25)

Not everyone who says to me, "Lord, Lord," will enter the kingdom of heaven, but only he who does the will of my Father who is in heaven. (Matthew 7:21)

Whoever acknowledges me before men, I will also acknowledge him before my Father in heaven. (Matthew 10:32)

Love your enemies, do good to them, and lend to them without expecting to get anything back. Then your reward will be great, and you will be sons of the Most High, because he is kind to the ungrateful and wicked. (Luke 6:35)

## PROMISES ABOUT PERSONAL FULFILLMENT

Whoever drinks the water I give him will never thirst. Indeed, the water I give him will become in him a spring of water welling up to eternal life. (John 4:14)

Whoever believes in me, as the Scripture has said, streams of living water will flow from within him. (John 7:38)

I am the gate; whoever enters through me will be saved. He will come in and go out, and find pasture. (John 10:9)

If you obey my commands, you will remain in my love, just as I have obeyed my Father's commands and remain in his love. I have told you this so that my joy may be in you and that your joy may be complete. (John 15:10–11)

Blessed are those who hunger and thirst for righteousness, for they will be filled. Blessed are the merciful, for they will be shown mercy. (Matthew 5:6–7)

But seek first his kingdom and his righteousness, and all these things will be given to you as well. (Matthew 6:33)

Come to me, all you who are weary and burdened, and I will give you rest. (Matthew 11:28)

## PROMISES ABOUT SECURITY

Everyone who hears these words of mine and puts them into practice is like a wise man who built his house on the rock. The rain came down, the streams rose, and the winds blew and beat against that house; yet it did not fall, because it had its foundation on the rock. (Matthew 7:24–25)

All that the Father gives me will come to me, and whoever comes to me I will never drive away. (John 6:37)

My sheep listen to my voice; I know them, and they follow me. I give them eternal life, and they shall never perish; no one can snatch them out of my hand. (John 10:27–28)

## PROMISES ABOUT INTIMACY WITH GOD

Whoever has my commands and obeys them, he is the one who loves me. He who loves me will be loved by my Father, and I too will love him and show myself to him. (John 14:21)

If anyone loves me, he will obey my teaching. My
Father will love him, and we will come to him and
make our home with him. (John 14:23)

If you obey my commands, you will remain in my
love, just as I have obeyed my Father's commands
and remain in his love. (John 15:10)

If a man remains in me and I in him, he will bear
much fruit; apart from me you can do nothing.
(John 15:5)

## PROMISES ABOUT TRUTH AND RIGHTEOUSNESS

I am the light of the world. Whoever follows me will
never walk in darkness, but will have the light of life.
(John 8:12)

If you abide in My word,…you shall know the truth,
and the truth shall make you free. (John 8:31–32,
NKJV)

I have come into the world as a light, so that no one who believes in me should stay in darkness. (John 12:46)

## PROMISES
## ABOUT DISCIPLESHIP

To the Jews who had believed him, Jesus said, "If you hold to my teaching, you are really my disciples. Then you will know the truth, and the truth will set you free." (John 8:31–32)

Whoever serves me must follow me; and where I am, my servant also will be. My Father will honor the one who serves me. (John 12:26)

Everyone who has left houses or brothers or sisters or father or mother or children or fields for my sake will receive a hundred times as much and will inherit eternal life. (Matthew 19:29)

## PROMISES
## ABOUT PRAYER

I will do whatever you ask in my name, so that the Son may bring glory to the Father. You may ask me for anything in my name, and I will do it. (John 14:13–14)

You did not choose me, but I chose you and appointed you to go and bear fruit—fruit that will last. Then the Father will give you whatever you ask in my name. (John 15:16)

In that day you will no longer ask me anything. I tell you the truth, my Father will give you whatever you ask in my name. Until now you have not asked for anything in my name. Ask and you will receive, and your joy will be complete. (John 16:23–24)

Where two or three come together in my name, there am I with them. (Matthew 18:20)

## PROMISES ABOUT THE HOLY SPIRIT

The Counselor, the Holy Spirit, whom the Father will send in my name, will teach you all things and will remind you of everything I have said to you. (John 14:26)

When he, the Spirit of truth, comes, he will guide you into all truth. He will not speak on his own; he will speak only what he hears, and he will tell you what is yet to come. (John 16:13)

If you then, though you are evil, know how to give good gifts to your children, how much more will your Father in heaven give the Holy Spirit to those who ask him! (Luke 11:13)

The promises Jesus made to His followers that we have not looked at here are just as glorious as these. You can find the complete list of Jesus's promises on pages 298–304 of *The Greatest Words Ever Spoken*.[8]

# APPENDIX

1. You will become His true disciple (John 8:31).
2. You will receive knowledge of the truth (John 8:32).
3. You will be liberated from enslavement to sin (John 8:34–36).
4. You will gain intimacy with Jesus the Son and God the Father (John 14:21).
5. You will be loved by the Father and the Son in a special way (John 14:21).
6. Jesus will reveal Himself to you (John 14:21).
7. The Father and the Son will come to you (John 14:23).
8. The Father and the Son will make their home with you (John 14:23).

9. You will be cleansed from your sin (John 15:3).

10. Your prayers will be answered (John 15:7).

11. You will bear much eternal fruit (John 15:8).

12. You will dwell (or remain) in Jesus's love (John 15:10).

13. Jesus's joy will be in you (John 15:11).

14. Your joy will be full (complete, overflowing) (John 15:11).

15. Your "house" (life) will not be destroyed (Matthew 7:25).

16. Your life will be built on the perfect foundation (Matthew 7:24; Luke 6:48).

17. You will be intimately known by Him (Matthew 7:21–25).

18. You will have assurance of your eternal life (Luke 6:46–48).

19. Your life and faith will not be shaken (Luke 6:48).

20. You'll have an ongoing infusion of spirit and life (John 6:63).

# NOTES

1. To find more information about this program, go to www.KnowingHim.org.

2. Frank Newport, Gallup News Service, "Americans More Likely to Believe in God Than the Devil, Heaven More Than Hell; Belief in the Devil Has Increased Since 2000," June 13, 2007, www.gallup.com/poll/27877/americans-more-likely-believe-god-than-devil-heaven-more-than-hell.aspx.

3. A note to pastors: Do you feel caught between a rock and a hard place? Does your heart's desire to focus on the realities of following Christ keep getting crowded out by church programs, the expectations and demands of your board and members, or the church's mortgage and budgetary needs? You don't need to bring radical changes overnight. Instead, focus on a gradual transition where your priorities shift more

and more toward teaching your people how to follow Christ.

4. A note to those in the pews: Just because your church is steeped in activities and programs doesn't mean you have to go in search of a different church. Work with your pastor and others to begin to transition the congregation's focus and priorities away from programs, so you can start to discover and obey what Jesus taught.

5. Elisabeth Elliot, *Shadow of the Almighty: The Life and Testament of Jim Elliot* (New York: Harper and Row, 1958), 15.

6. Steven K. Scott, *The Greatest Words Ever Spoken: Everything Jesus Said About You, Your Life, and Everything Else* (Colorado Springs, CO: WaterBrook, 2008), 206–17.

7. Keep in mind that a casual understanding of Jesus's commands or mere intellectual agreement with His teachings does not constitute *belief* as that word is used in Scripture. The Greek word for "belief"—*pisteuo*—means to "totally trust, rely upon, and commit to."

8. Scott, *Greatest Words,* 298–304.

# EVERYTHING JESUS SAID.
# PERIOD

More than 1,900 statements of Jesus organized under more than 200 topics

## THE GREATEST
## WORDS
## EVER SPOKEN

EVERYTHING JESUS SAID ABOUT YOU,
YOUR LIFE, AND EVERYTHING ELSE

FOREWORD BY GARY SMALLEY

### STEVEN K. SCOTT

AUTHOR OF *The Richest Man Who Ever Lived*

*The Greatest Words Ever Spoken* offers you a fast, easy way to find everything Jesus said about hundreds of issues that are crucial to your life, relationships, faith, and spiritual growth.

**Read an excerpt from this book and more at**
**www.WaterBrookMultnomah.com!**

# LEARN THE SECRETS TO SUCCESS AND SIGNIFICANCE FROM THE LIFE OF JESUS

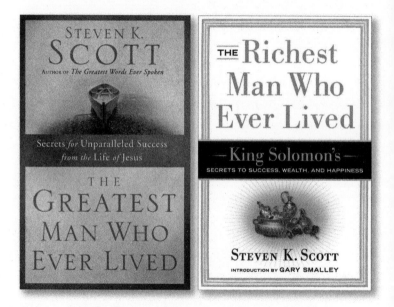

Multimillionaire entrepreneur Steven K. Scott explores and applies the biblical wisdom of Jesus' life to mentor you into a life of extraordinary personal, relational, spiritual, and financial success.

**Read an excerpt from these books and more at**
**www.WaterBrookMultnomah.com!**